# CONSIDER IT JOY

A SIX-MONTH GUIDED BULLET JOURNAL

BY CANDACE PAYNE

BELLE CITY GIFTS

Belle City Gifts
Savage, Minnesota, USA

Belle City Gifts is an imprint of BroadStreet Publishing® Group, LLC.
Broadstreetpublishing.com

*Consider It Joy*

ISBN 978-1-4245-5779-0

Author is represented by Icon Management Group,
http://iconmgmtgroup.com.

Design by Chris Garborg | garborgdesign.com
Editorial services by Michelle Winger | literallyprecise.com

Printed in China.

18   19   20   21   22   23   24      7   6   5   4   3   2   1

# Introduction

Hey there! I am so glad you got this journal! *Consider It Joy* is the favorite thing I have made to help people live a life full of joy.

If you're anything like me, you have a hard time seeing progress and setting goals in your joy journey. It's one thing to hope for more joy, and another thing to pursue it. It took me a long time to realize I had a choice to pursue joy the same way I pursued my goals.

This guided bullet journal is not just a pretty six-month project. It is a place where you can fight and fuss and be as honest as you want about every aspect of your life. It is a toolbox to help you make margin and space for joy every day. It can serve as a gauge for where you are, and a map to chart where you long to be.

So, join me, won't you? Get as crazy and crafty as your inspiration will let you. Just stay the course. Open this journal. And, no matter what happens in these next six months, *Consider It Joy*.

Your Biggest Cheerleader,

# UNLOCK YOUR

THE KEY YOU NEED

*Joy*

| | | | | | | |
|---|---|---|---|---|---|---|
| ☐ | TASK | ○ | EVENT | ♡ | WORKOUT |
| ⊠ | COMPLETED TASK | ⊗ | COMPLETED EVENT | 🎂 | BIRTHDAY |
| → | FORWARDED TASK | ① | PRIORITY EVENT | $ | MONEY RELATED |
| ⊟ | DELETED TASK | ⊖ | DELETED EVENT | ☁ | INSPIRATION |
| ! | PRIORITY TASK | • | NOTE | | |
| ◪ | TASK IN PROGRESS | ? | RESEARCH FURTHER | | |

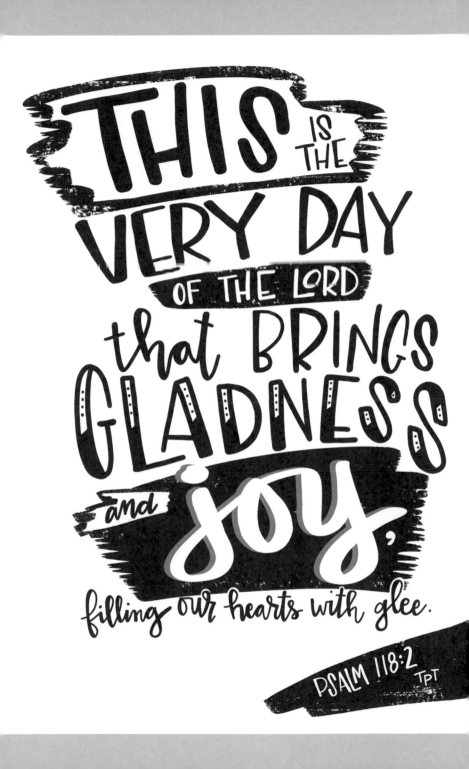

_Month:_ _____

| SUNDAY | MONDAY | TUESDAY | WEDNESDAY |
|--------|--------|---------|-----------|
|        |        |         |           |
|        |        |         |           |
|        |        |         |           |
|        |        |         |           |
|        |        |         |           |
|        |        |         |           |

| THURSDAY | FRIDAY | SATURDAY | TASKS/ GOALS |
|---|---|---|---|
|  |  |  |  |
|  |  |  |  |
|  |  |  |  |
|  |  |  |  |
|  |  |  |  |
|  |  |  |  |

# What Can Happen in a Day

In the middle of one of the most chaotic seasons of my life, I discovered a quote that changed *everything*. It was a Wednesday evening at my local church in a mid-week service. I was overwhelmed, exhausted, and spent. Honestly, I felt like going to a spa and getting my feet soaked and nails manicured instead of pretending I was engaged in what was happening. I knew the only reason I was there was because my kids were involved in their own activities that they loved. It was too late to retreat to my car with my phone and latest Netflix episode to inhale a bag of Doritos because I had been spotted by one of the church staff. "Dang. Now I gotta go."

I remember walking in the room physically but checking out mentally. All I wanted was some rest. All I *needed* was some rest. I had been burning myself out at both ends in my effort to do incredible, "holy" things. I was devoid of happiness. Joy was the last thing on my list. I had an unspoken expectation that I would get joy as a reward for the energy I was spending on the task.

I waited through song after song for the cue to sit down. Worship felt more like a glorified playlist than an encounter with the living God. I was checked out, y'all. I started listening when I heard my pastor jump on stage and begin to talk about time management. At first, I thought, "Great. Now God is going to lecture me on how I am doing it all wrong." (Please tell me you've had these thoughts as well? I can't actually hear you agreeing, but I'm going to confidently assume you're nodding your head.)

My pastor made several good points, I am sure of it. But I can only remember one phrase—the phrase that changed how I approach every day. It leapt out of his mouth and kicked me right in the gut: **"Would God give you all the talent, creativity, and gifts you need to do what He asks and not give you enough time to do it?"** My mind began racing. If that were true, God would be cruel. It would not match what I knew of Him through Scripture. Even more difficult to grasp was that if the statement was not true, I needed to evaluate what I was doing with my days.

There is a difference between doing something "good" and doing something "God." I started to list on the back of an offering envelope all the things I had done that day and all I had yet to accomplish. Many seemed like "good" things. However, when I took a harder look, many were not "God" things—things I had prayed about doing to bring Him glory. If I am being honest at a level that brings me much embarrassment, they were things that made me feel better about myself, shrouded in false humility. They were, in all sense of the word, distractions.

I love how Psalm 118 puts it:

*This is the very day of the Lord that brings gladness and joy, filling our hearts with glee.*

PSALM 118:2 TPT

I had forgotten every day is God's day. When I am doing God days with Him at the center of every to-do list, I find joy. I can't explain how I delight in folding a pile of towels, or grabbing school lunch supplies, I just do. I look for where God is leading me. Who is He putting beside me in the checkout line that needs a smile? Sometimes, He nudges me to pay for someone's coffee or buy a tank of gas for the neighbor at the pump. When I remember that the day is God's, it's always better. He gives me the perfect amount of time to do everything. My reward is not joy at the end of my task but right there in the dead center of doing it.

This month, I encourage you to spend each day looking back at this verse. Read it out loud. Commit it to memory. Make a cute paperclip bookmark on this page so you open here first. Whatever it takes, get it in your heart that every day is from God and for Him. Through Him, you will find your joy! This is your first challenge in knowing how to *consider it joy.*

# VISION BOARD

FOR THE MONTH OF: _____

GOALS

GOALS

GOALS

GOALS

# think

## ON THESE THINGS...

USE THIS SPACE TO WRITE YOUR FAVORITE PASSAGES AND QUOTES.

WRITE THE TITLE [ON THE SPINES] OF BOOKS YOU WANT TO READ. [COLOR THE BOOK ONCE YOU'VE READ IT.]

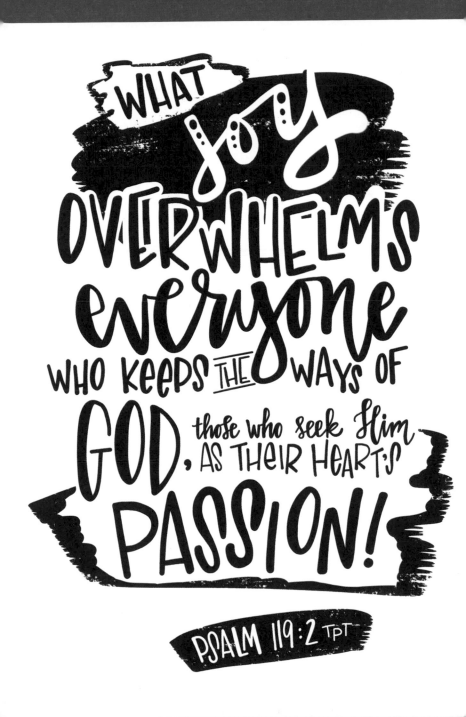

WHAT JOY OVERWHELMS EVERYONE WHO KEEPS THE WAYS OF GOD, those who seek Him, AS THEIR HEART'S PASSION!

PSALM 119:2 TPT

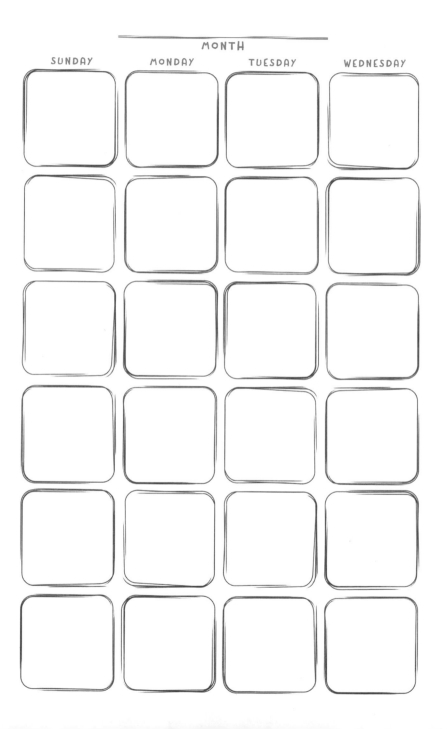

MONTH

| SUNDAY | MONDAY | TUESDAY | WEDNESDAY |

THURSDAY

FRIDAY

SATURDAY

TASKS/
GOALS

# Losing My Way

The moment I remember losing my way is one of my favorite moments. I'm not being sarcastic. I know it's hard to tell if you know me well. After all, I believe that sarcasm could very well be a love language. But, seriously. The day I lost my way was one of the most instrumental moments to increasing my faith and sustaining my joy. How could my faith grow and my joy remain from losing my way? I am not speaking of losing my way in the context we usually speak of. Look again at the passage that I highlighted this month.

*What joy overwhelms everyone who keeps the way of God, those who seek him as their heart's passion!*
PSALM 119:2 TPT

It was a Tuesday evening in the middle of exam week during my third year of college. I was having a meltdown, cramming information I was sure to never retain once testing was over. I was over-extended in both school and social commitments, and consumed with being perfect. Perfection became my one and only passionate aim. If I wasn't the best at everything, I would try until my body was exhausted and sick. Perfection pursuits whittle your body, mind, and soul to mere rubble if left unchecked. I was broken that night as I began to pray.

At the time, I had become very legalistic in my faith. Even if I needed sleep, I wouldn't go to bed until I read my Bible and prayed. It looked like I was doing a really good thing, but I was doing it my way… in my own strength. (FYI—I've discovered one of the most holy things you can ever do is shut up, lay down, and take a nap. Can I get an "Amen"?!)

Through my frustration of trying to be perfect and pleasing to God, my prayers got a bit loud and intense. I remember trying to check off my list: read the Bible passage, give thanks for answered prayer, praise God… but something violently switched in me. I broke down in tears. I know it was both from physical exhaustion and spiritual dissatisfaction. And, I knew it was long overdue. When I could finally begin to put words together again, all I could say was, *"God, I am so tired of never being good enough! What's worse, I'm afraid I'll never be good enough for you!"*

When I sat in those words as they fell to the ground, I heard the Spirit of God speak these words in response: *"I'm so glad you finally realize you can never be good enough."*

**I had been trying to live for God without God.** It sucked. Like, literally, it sucked all the joy and passion out of my life. I was convinced, for the first time, I had to lose my way in order to regain my joy and passion.

I love how this month's verse speaks the truth so perfectly. Joy overwhelms us when we lose our way and keep God's way. Our very best is never good enough. It wasn't meant to be. If it were, there would be no need for Jesus, salvation, or hope. If I could earn anything on my own, I wouldn't be in need of everything. Our right-ness with God is only because of His Son, Jesus.

If you're really on a journey to *consider it joy* in every circumstance, you must lose your way. I'd dare say you've struggled a long while with very little enjoyment along the way. The joy you're longing for must first be found in losing something you thought was helping.

Don't be afraid to lose your way. Make God's way your only way. I've discovered how overwhelming joy can be in His process and perfection, and I know you can find it too!

Commit this verse to memory this month as you find yourself following familiar paths. If it takes every single day of losing your way, do it. It'll be your joy before you know it.

TASKS

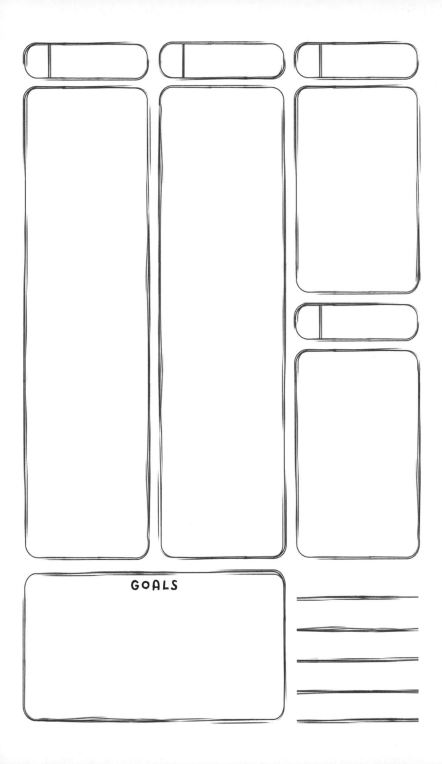

GOALS

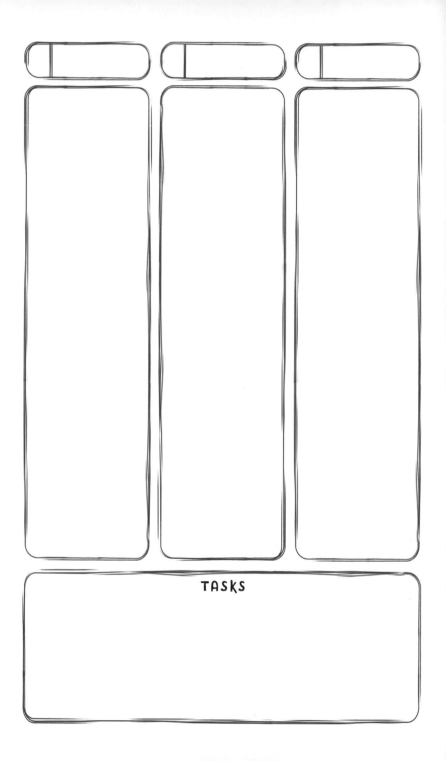

TASKS

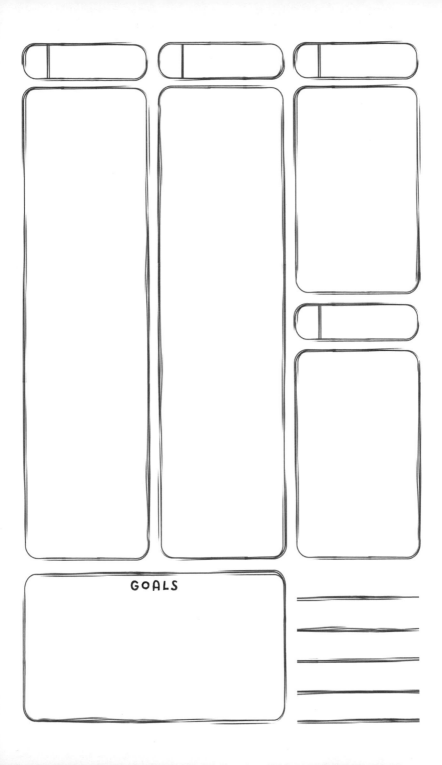

GOALS

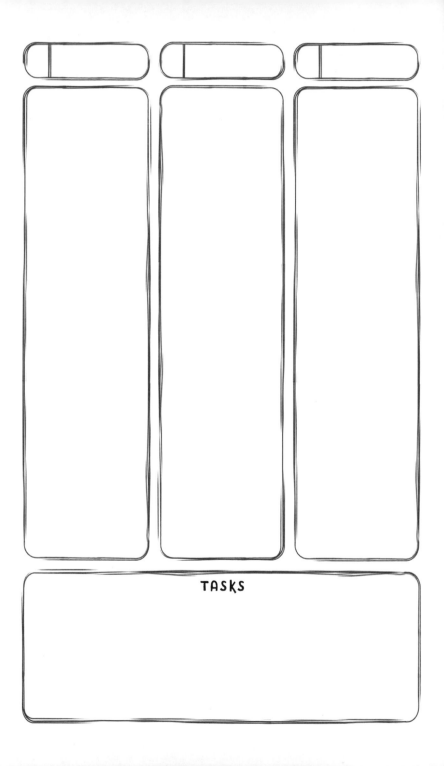

TASKS

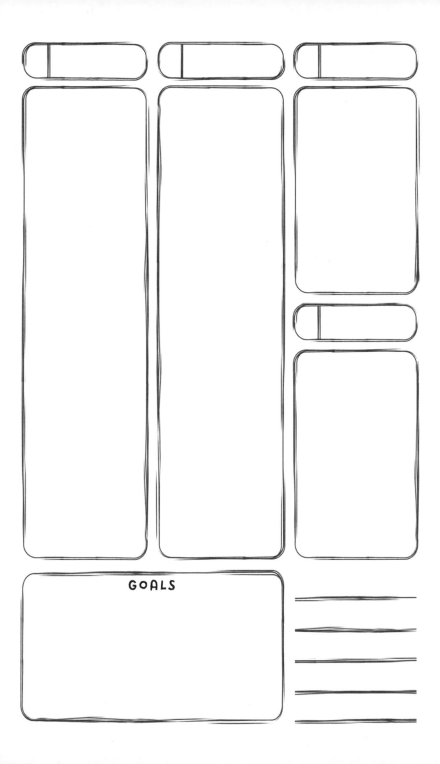

GOALS

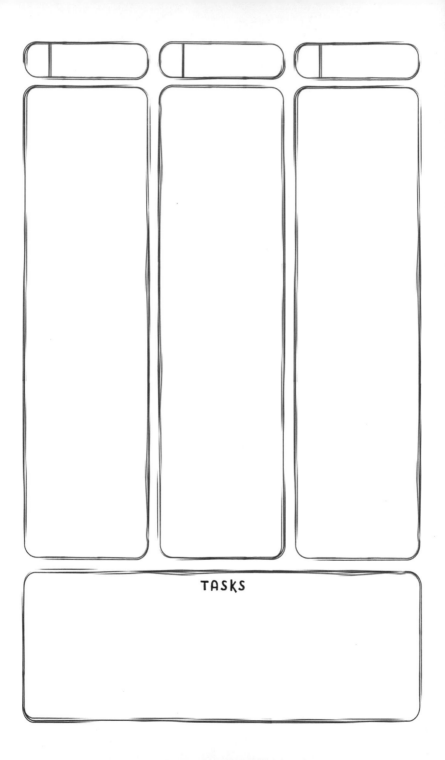

TASKS

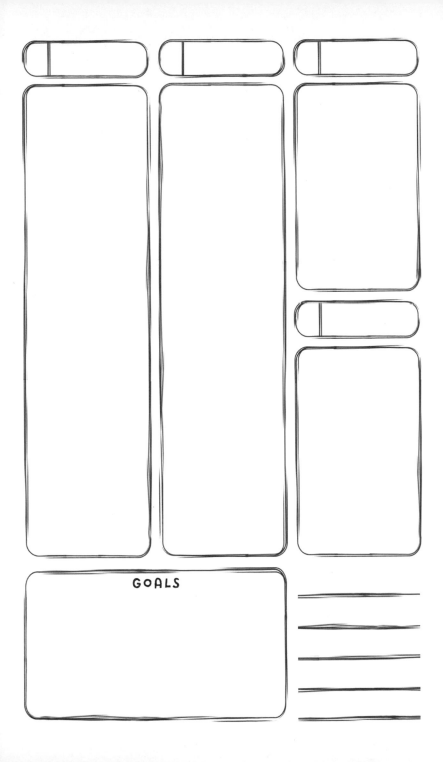

GOALS

# VISION-BOARD

FOR THE MONTH OF: _____

Month:

| Sunday | Monday | Tuesday | Wednesday |
|--------|--------|---------|-----------|
|        |        |         |           |
|        |        |         |           |
|        |        |         |           |
|        |        |         |           |
|        |        |         |           |
|        |        |         |           |

| Thursday | Friday | Saturday |
| --- | --- | --- |
| | | |

Tasks

Goals

# VISION BOARD

## FOR THE MONTH OF:_____

# When Fear Flees and Joy Floods

*Then my fears will dissolve into limitless joy*
*because of Your mighty deliverance.*

PSALM 35:9 TPT

I cannot tell you how often fear is a nemesis to experiencing a life full of joy. In our pursuit together to make every day a consideration in how we find joy, we cannot let this enemy lie undetected. Fear finds us all. It manifests itself in many different ways. To some it looks like control, to others anger, and to many it begins building walls for a sense of security. We all respond differently when fear rises up.

Because God stands to deliver us, we can see the promise in this passage: our fears can dissolve into joy. And, not just joy, but *limitless* joy. How incredible would it be to see joy without limit bombard our fears? In order to see that, we must be dependent.

I think our visceral reaction to fear is to take it upon ourselves to devise a plan, stand a bit taller, or cave in. This is the opposite of what we need most in the middle of our fear. Perfect love casts out fear. In Psalm 23, we see this phrase:

*The comfort of your love takes away my fear.*

PSALM 23:4 TPT

There is a God much bigger than your fears. I am not just talking about fears of darkness, spiders, or creepy clowns. Internal fears of being alone, failing, or losing all you have are also included. God knows the things you question silently. *He knows.* His perfect love comes to the rescue.

More often than not, fear is trust in something that may or may not ever exist. When we begin to trust in the unfailing love of God, we will not be shaken. And even more, we stand to see our fears dissolve into limitless joy. There is joy in trusting.

Do you see the correlation? *Love fuels trust.* Trust, then, fuels joy. Fear cannot have a hold in either place.

I want to ask you to do something a bit different this month. This assignment is something that began to uncover fear and expose truth in my personal walk with God. I was challenged to write out my fears on one page, then write the very words of God (Scripture) that fights that specific fear on the page adjacent to it.

I love y'all so much that I've started the pages for you. All you have to do is be faithful to expose your fear when you feel it. Then dig. Dive into the Word of God with a good old concordance or use Google to find a verse that speaks the opposite of your fear.

This month, let's watch those fears flee into puddles of possibility for endless joy.

It's going to take some hard work and honesty, but trust that God loves you and wants you to know limitless joy as much as you do.

You've got this!

my fears

# GOD's PROMISES

Tasks

Goals

Tasks

Goals

Tasks

Goals

Tasks

Goals

# MONTH

| SUNDAY | MONDAY | TUESDAY | WEDNESDAY |

| THURSDAY | FRIDAY | SATURDAY | TASKS |
|----------|--------|----------|-------|

# VISION BOARD

## FOR THE MONTH OF: _____

FIGHT with JOY.

COLOR the EMPTY SPACES in the word "JOY" EACH DAY YOU FIGHT back with joy.

# Restore

One thing I know about the pursuit for joy is this: there must be action. It is so easy to expect joy to just happen to us. Yet, when we look at this word *restore*, we see that it is indeed a verb. It means bringing back, returning, repairing, renovating, or giving back. We have the tendency to believe that our joy is dependent on our work. But, if you look closely at the passage below, it is a prayer for God to do the work. As a matter of fact, the only work that is described as belonging to us is serving a good God.

> *Restore joy to your loving servant once again,*
> *for all I am is yours, O God.*
> PSALM 86:4 TPT

Can I free you up from some incredibly cumbersome thinking? It's not your job to restore your joy. As a matter of fact, it's not possible to obtain true joy outside of the very Spirit of God. I know that sounds like a bold statement, but the Apostle Paul tells us clearly:

> *The fruit produced by the Holy Spirit within you is divine*
> *love in all its varied expressions:*
> *joy that overflows, peace that subdues,*
> *patience that endures, kindness in action,*
> *a life full of virtue, faith that prevails,*
> *gentleness of heart, and strength of spirit.*
> GALATIANS 5:22-23 TPT

The Spirit of God at work in you produces the joy you are longing for. The only requirement is that we belong to Him.

Think of it this way:
Someone sets out to buy a home in less than perfect condition—a fixer upper, if you will. They pay for the home. Then, they go in and inspect where improvements or repairs are needed to get the home back in good condition. They begin the work of gutting and bringing in new materials. Before you know it, the house that once looked dilapidated and nearly condemned is more beautiful than it ever was before.

You were bought at a very high price through the life that Jesus, God's Son, gave on a brutal cross. You and I both are fixer uppers. We cannot fix ourselves. It takes the work of the One who purchased our lives to restore us to our original design... and then some!

If you find yourself tired in your pursuit of joy, here is some much needed relief: you're the renovation, not the Renovator. Rest in the process of what the Master Builder is designing in you. How?

*"As you live in union with me as your source, fruitfulness will stream from within you—but when you live separated from me you are powerless."*

JOHN 15:5 TPT

Remain in God. Stay right in the center of who He is and what He is doing. You will soon see your joy restored in ways that you never knew possible.

This month, find time to identify things you are trying to do without the help of God. Are there areas of your life that need to be joined with the Father again? Remember, Jesus said that apart from Him you are powerless. Is there a specific area where you feel you are spinning your wheels? Maybe you are repeating behaviors without any positive results. Pray through these areas and join them with the Father.

Remember, all you are is God's. What better place to be than in Him? He is the provider and restorer of your joy. When you give your life to Him, you can trust that He will do better with it than you can do on your own.

I'm excited for your joy journey this month. I love how freeing it is when we accept the helping hands of the Father.

TASKS

GOALS

_____

_____

_____

_____

_____

## TASKS

GOALS

TASKS

GOALS

TASKS

GOALS

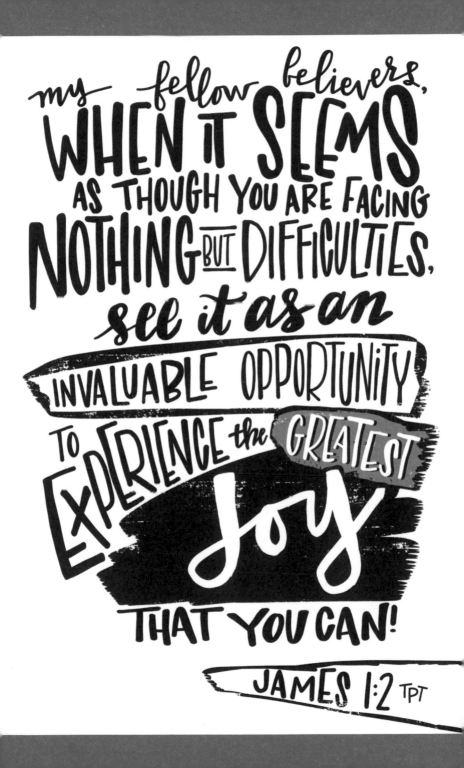

Month:

~~~~~~~~~~~~~~~~~~~~~~~~~~~~~~~~~~~~

| SUNDAY | MONDAY | TUESDAY | WEDNESDAY |
|--------|--------|---------|-----------|
|        |        |         |           |
|        |        |         |           |
|        |        |         |           |
|        |        |         |           |
|        |        |         |           |
|        |        |         |           |

| THURSDAY | FRIDAY | SATURDAY | TASKS/ GOALS |
|----------|--------|----------|--------------|
|          |        |          |              |
|          |        |          |              |
|          |        |          |              |
|          |        |          |              |
|          |        |          |              |
|          |        |          |              |

# VISION BOARD

FOR THE MONTH OF:_____

# Invaluable Opportunity

*My fellow believers, when it seems as though you are facing nothing but difficulties, see it as an invaluable opportunity to experience the greatest joy that you can.*

JAMES 1:2 TPT

Most often, I see difficulties and troubles as distractions and detours. Rarely do I see them as opportunities—let alone, an opportunity for joy. If you're anything like me, when things don't go as planned you find yourself scrambling to make it work or trying to pull yourself out of whatever mess you're in. Heaven forbid you have to interact with others in a pleasant manner while you are attempting to stay afloat.

Some of my most embarrassing moments have been witnessed in how I treat others when expectations are crashed with a reality that is more difficult or unexpected. I become short tempered, sharp tongued, and miserable company. Yet, this seems to be the exact opposite of how we should respond. Y'all, this may be the hardest concept to grasp about joy yet.

Look at the very first words in this month's passage: "My fellow **believers**…" That alone makes me pause and ask, "What do I really believe?" Is God good? Does He care about my life and my desires? Does He care about my family and my health? Does He love me?

The answers to what I believe about God and what His Word says fuels my response toward difficulties. I don't think we can fake what we really believe. Think of it this way: If I say that I believe a metal folding chair can sustain my weight and balance my body when I sit in it, I'll prove it to be true by actually sitting in the chair.

Many times we say we trust and believe God to be good, caring, and for us, but we never rest in those beliefs when we need to the most. I don't think it's even possible to see an opportunity for joy when your belief system about God is compromised.

**Trust fuels joy.**

I am not going to ask you to jump right into finding joy in the worst report you've heard from a doctor. I am not asking you to put on a fake smile and pretend to find great joy in the middle of your deepest sorrows. But, I am asking that you believe it to be possible. Let's at least start there.

This month, I want you to list out the "non-negotiables" of your belief in God. These should all come from the very Word of God. For example, if I said that God is loving, I would find Scriptures that support that. There are several that come to mind, but for example's sake, here's just one:

*We have come into an intimate experience with God's love,
and we trust in the love he has for us. God is love!
Those who are living in love are living in God,
and God lives through them.*
1 JOHN 4:16 TPT

Make your list of what you genuinely believe to be true about the character of God. Then, make a list of Scriptures that reflect those beliefs to be true.

Soon, I hope you'll begin to see difficulties and troubles turn from distractions into opportunities for great joy! When you can believe in a good God, you can consider it all joy... no matter what comes.

Goals

Goals

LET

Joy

BE YOUR

CONTINUAL

FEAST.

1 THESSALONIANS 5:16 TPT

# MONTH

◇◇◇◇◇◇◇◇◇◇◇◇◇◇◇◇◇◇◇◇◇◇◇◇◇◇◇◇◇◇◇◇◇◇◇

| SUNDAY | MONDAY | TUESDAY | WEDNESDAY |
|--------|--------|---------|-----------|

◇◇◇◇◇◇◇◇◇◇◇◇◇◇◇◇◇◇◇◇◇◇◇◇◇◇◇◇◇◇◇◇◇◇◇

THURSDAY

FRIDAY

SATURDAY

TASKS

GOALS

# Edible Joy

Have you ever heard the old phrase, "You are what you eat"? I am basically a walking taco at this moment in my life. Tacos for the win! Like, who doesn't love a good taco? Are you human, even?

There's a deeper reality to this old adage. What you put in your body to fuel it can heal or destroy it. Over the years, I have had to learn to add green vegetables to my diet, drink more than just lattés and sweet tea (i.e. water), and try things that I don't even know how to pronounce. Try reading this word out loud and tell me if you pronounce it right: *quinoa*. Y'all, healthy ain't easy. Oh, the simplicity of driving through a restaurant and grabbing a paper bag of greasy nuggets, cheeseburgers, and French fries! But, if that is your only diet, you find yourself packing on extra pounds, clogging arteries, and destroying the insides of your body. You do become what you eat… eventually.

I love how this verse encourages us to feast on joy!

*Let joy be your continual feast.*
1 THESSALONIANS 5:16 TPT

I see joy as one of those things that sometimes isn't easy to take in. It's often easier to look at situations pessimistically and complain. Lord knows, my visceral response in almost every situation is laced with pride and self-pity.

Joy is the choice made that tastes *fresh*. The more I started eating healthy foods, the more I began to crave them. The more my body received water instead of soda, the more deficient I felt when I wasn't making good choices. Joy is similar in many ways. It may have a different taste than you're used to at first. I get it. It's not easy to respond with joy as your first reaction. But the more you feast, the more you crave. The more joy you put in, the more it becomes a reaction instead of a discipline.

How do you feast on joy? Take what you've learned in these past few months about letting the Spirit of God own every part of your life and keep putting it into action. Whenever you feel as though you are hard pressed or crushed, return to the truth of God's goodness in every situation. Read and re-read the pages of this journal where you have fought to find joy and truth. Release fears and control when you feel the urge to return to familiar paths of apathy and shame.

Keep choosing joy every day.

Consider joy when you cannot see it in your circumstance.

Stay hungry for joy.

Soon, joy will be a part of your very character, not just a distant want.

Set an alarm every day this month around your lunch break. When you hear the sound, remember to feast on joy. Look through these pages. Hide Scriptures in your heart. Cultivate gratitude. Find ways to give to those less fortunate.

Above all… never stop gobbling up joy. It's the good stuff that keeps you healthy and strong. How do I know? The Bible tells me so.

*The joy of the Lord is your strength.*
NEHEMIAH 8:10 ESV

TASKS

GOALS

TASKS

GOALS

TASKS

GOALS

TASKS

GOALS

# VISION BOARD

FOR THE MONTH OF:_____

Candace Payne is an author, speaker and viral sensation. Her 2016 Facebook Live video, which shows her trying on a Chewbacca Mask, holds the record for the most-viewed Facebook Live video in history (170+ million views) and resulted in her becoming internationally known as "Chewbacca Mom." She has been featured in more than 3,000 media outlets including "Good Morning America," "The Late Late Show with James Corden," *The New York Times*, *PEOPLE*, and *Cosmopolitan*. Candace is the author of three books and a small group curriculum. She lives in Texas with her husband, two children, and ornery pugs.